PUPPETS

Meryl Doney

Franklin Watts
A Division of Grolier Publishing
New York ● London ● Hong Kong ● Sydney
Danbury, Connecticut

About this book

In this book you will find examples of puppets from a wide variety of countries and backgrounds. The puppet theater of each country has its own distinctive style, with different designs, colors, and traditions. When you have decided which puppets you would like to make, begin by looking at the relevant maps to see where the puppets come from.

Try to find other books on the particular countries and their culture, and read all about them. When you are ready to decorate your puppets, the theater, and props, use traditional designs or patterns copied from these reference books. This will help to make your puppet theater more like the real thing.

Adapt the ideas from this book freely as you go along, and invent your own puppet characters.

Most of the steps are very easy to follow, but where you see this sign it is best to ask for help from an adult.

Performing plays

Many puppet performances around the world take place in the open air, with a minimum amount of equipment. This makes the puppets very easy to use. On pages 28–29 you will find some notes on staging plays in this way, with instructions for building three simple stages. There is also a play idea in which all the puppets in this book can appear.

When you have made your characters, you may prefer to develop a traditional play for them to perform. Such plays are usually drawn from the history of a particular country, from traditional fables, religious stories, or moral tales. Your local library will have a good collection of stories from around the world, and you can simplify and adapt them to suit the puppets you have made.

First published in the United States in 1995 by Franklin Watts
Text © 1995 by Meryl Doney

Franklin Watts
95 Madison Ave
New York, NY 10016

10 9 8 7 6 5 4 3 2 1

Series editor: Annabel Martin
Editor: Jane Walker
Design: Visual Image
Cover design: Chloë Cheesman/Mike Davis
Artwork: Ruth Levy
Photography: Peter Millard

With special thanks to Alison Croft, educational advisor and puppet maker.

Library of Congress Cataloging-in-Publication Data:
Doney, Meryl, 1942 –
    Puppets/Meryl Doney.
        p.   cm. – (World crafts)
    Includes bibliographical references and index.
    ISBN 0-531-14399-6 (lib. bdg.)
    1. Puppet making – Juvenile literature.
    2. Puppets – Juvenile literature. [1. Puppets.
    2. Puppet making. 3. Handicraft.]
    I. Title II. Series.
    TT174.7.D66 1995   95-11433
    745.592'24 – dc20   CIP AC

Printed in Great Britain

Contents

Puppet history

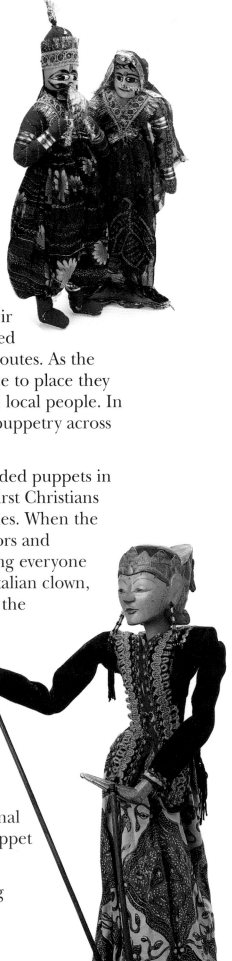

Traditional puppet theaters exist in almost every country in the world. One of the earliest puppets, a monkey character, was discovered in India and may be over 4,000 years old. There are also early records of plays about legendary heroes and gods being acted by shadow, rod, and marionette puppets in China and the Far East.

From these early beginnings in Asia, entertainers and their puppets probably traveled along the great trading routes. As the entertainers moved from place to place they would stop and perform for the local people. In this way they spread the art of puppetry across the ancient world.

The Greeks and Romans included puppets in their religious plays, and the first Christians used them to teach Bible stories. When the Roman Empire fell apart, actors and puppeteers again traveled across Europe entertaining everyone from kings to the crowds in the marketplace. The Italian clown, Polcinella, grew out of this tradition, and from him the Punchinello, or Punch, glove puppet evolved.

Puppets were brought to North America and Australia in the nineteenth century by emigrants from Europe. (There is some evidence that the North American Indians and Aboriginal peoples of Australia had their own puppet tradition before then.)

Today, puppets are more popular than ever. Many famous characters have been created for international TV programs such as "Sesame Street" and "The Muppet Show," as well as for feature films.

We hope you enjoy making your puppets and giving pleasure to others as you perform your own plays.

Your own puppet-making kit

As you begin making your puppets, look around for odd bits of material, buttons, cardboard tubes, and yogurt cups. Keep these items in a box with a set of tools ready for when you want to make a puppet.

Make some dough from the recipes below and store that too. Wrap it in plastic wrap and keep in a container with a tight lid.

Here are some of the most useful items for your puppet-making kit:

hammer • nail with a large head • small saw • needle-nose pliers • scissors • mat knife • metal ruler with cork on back • brushes • poster paints • gesso • paintbrush • white glue (like Elmer's) • modeling clay or Sculpey • masking tape • cardboard • oak tag •

paper • tissue paper • newspaper • pen • pencil • felt-tip pens • fabric and felt • needle and thread • decorations, including sequins, buttons, braid, aluminum foil, sticky shapes, beads • newspaper to work on • cardboard to cut on • apron • paper towels for cleaning up

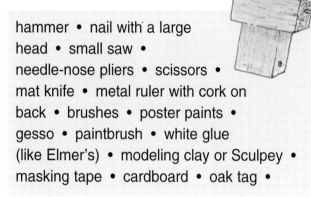

Potato dough

This dough recipe comes from Peru. It is made from mashed potatoes and plaster of Paris.

3 tablespoons of instant mashed potatoes
10 tablespoons of plaster of Paris
water

In a small bowl, mix the mashed potatoes with 1/4 pint of boiling water. Beat with a fork until floury.

In a larger bowl, mix the plaster with 3 tablespoons of cold water. Stir with an old spoon until smooth.

Add the potatoes to the plaster and mix well. Form into a dough and knead well.

No cooking is required for this dough.

Salt dough

2 cups of flour
1/2 cup of salt
3/4 cup of water

Mix the flour and salt together in a large bowl.

Make a well in the middle, pour in a little water, and stir with a fork. Keep adding water, a little at a time, until you have used it all.

Finish mixing and kneading the dough with your hands. If it is too sticky, add more flour; if too dry, add more water.

Salt dough must be dried in the oven to produce a hard result.

Dancing puppets

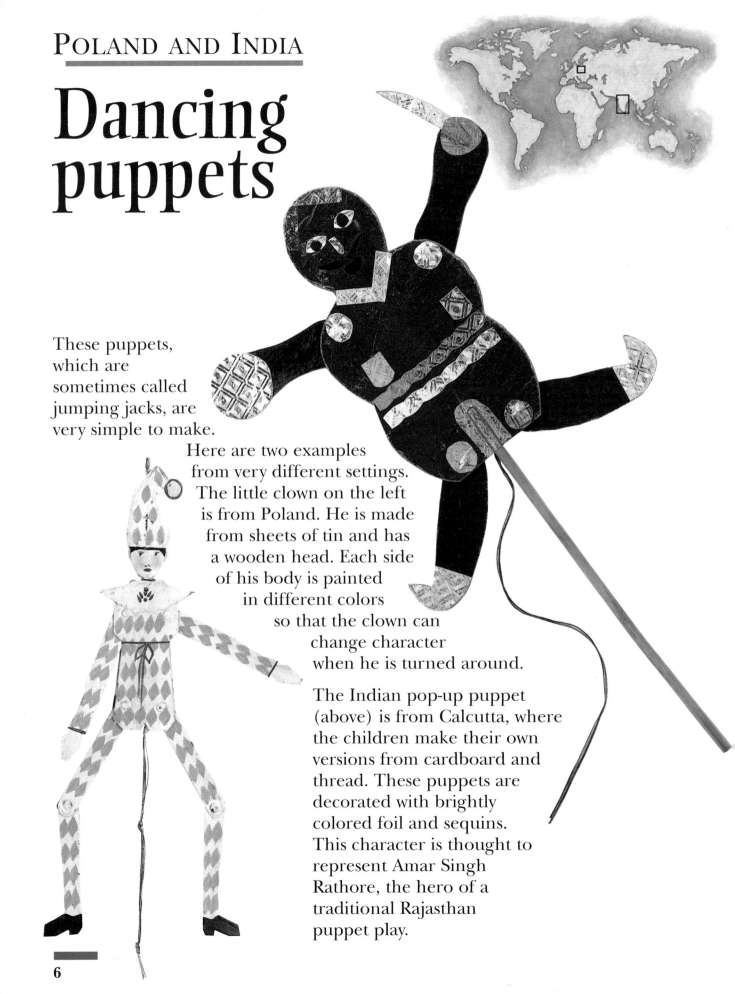

These puppets, which are sometimes called jumping jacks, are very simple to make.

Here are two examples from very different settings. The little clown on the left is from Poland. He is made from sheets of tin and has a wooden head. Each side of his body is painted in different colors so that the clown can change character when he is turned around.

The Indian pop-up puppet (above) is from Calcutta, where the children make their own versions from cardboard and thread. These puppets are decorated with brightly colored foil and sequins. This character is thought to represent Amar Singh Rathore, the hero of a traditional Rajasthan puppet play.

Make an Indian pop-up puppet

You will need: cardboard/ illustration board • aluminum foil • white glue • colored paper • needle and thread • a garden stick/chopstick • tape

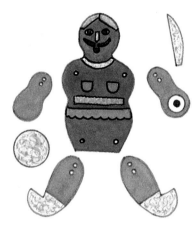

1 Cut simple body parts from cardboard. Glue on pieces of foil and colored paper to form face and uniform. Cover shield and saber with aluminum foil. Make two small holes in the top of each arm and leg. Make four holes in the body as shown.

2 Join arms together with thread. Use the holes that are nearest the edges. Knot at the back. Join legs in the same way.

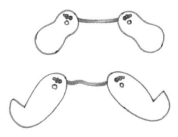

3 Attach arms to body with thread, using the bottom holes on the arms. Knot at the back and front. Attach legs in the same way.

4 Use another thread to join the arms and legs, so that you can make the puppet jump.

Cover the back by gluing a piece of colored paper onto the back of the neck.

5 Split the top $3/4$ in (2 cm) of a small, green garden stick. Push puppet into it and secure with tape. Neaten split end and knots by covering with aluminum foil. Attach shield and saber.

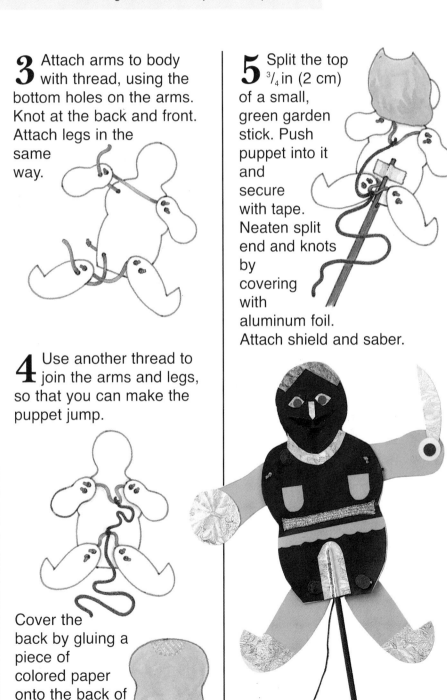

7

Hand puppets

China has a history of puppet making that goes back over 2,000 years. This glove puppet is based on the historic Ku Li Tzu puppet theater. The puppeteer carried his puppets from town to town in a small boxlike theater slung from the end of a pole. To begin the show, he would prop the pole against a wall and unroll curtains from below the stage to hide himself. After the show he would hoist the whole thing onto his shoulder again and move on to the next village.

Like the characters in Chinese opera, this puppet's face is painted to show his personality. He is a young man because he has no beard. You could make your puppet angry or sad, young or old, depending on the story you plan to perform. You may be able to find designs for faces in a book on Chinese opera.

Make a Ku Li Tzu puppet

You will need: salt dough (see recipe, page 5) · a cork · a potholder · paints · varnish · cardboard · white glue · colored fabric · white or beige fabric · ribbon · felt-tip pen · rice (uncooked)

1 To make the head, take a piece of dough about the size of a Ping-Pong ball. Push a cork into it and mold more dough around the cork to form the neck. Shape the chin and add small pieces of dough for the facial features.

2 For boots, roll two small sausage shapes. Bend into L-shapes, flatten soles, and point toes. Shape two smaller pieces of dough into hands. With the help of an adult, bake all dough shapes at 200°F (95°C) until hard (about 30 minutes). Remove cork and leave head to cool in oven.

3 Paint all the pieces white, then add color, and varnish.

4 Cut out four pieces from cardboard for the headdress. Glue rectangle around head, fold in sides, and staple at top. Glue on other pieces of cardboard and decorate.

front

back

5 Cut out fabric pieces for the robe. Pin and sew them, right sides together, leaving arm and neck holes. Hem. Decorate with felt-tip pen. Glue head and hands into the holes and turn robe the right side out. Trim the neck with ribbon.

Sewing hint: If you sew one way with running stitch, and then come back again filling in the spaces, you will make a strong seam.

6 Cut out front panel and hem around it. Decorate with felt-tip pen. Sew to front of robe. Make legs from two rectangles of white fabric. Sew up the sides to make tubes. Turn right side out and glue a boot into each tube. Fill legs with rice, leaving $1\frac{1}{2}$ in (4 cm) empty at top.

7 Fold in $\frac{1}{2}$ in (1 cm) of fabric and pin legs inside front of robe under panel. Sew.

9

Papier-mâché glove puppets

Punchinello, or Punch, as we know him today, is a puppet with a fascinating history. As far as we can discover, he began life in Italy as a funny character called Polcinella. Italian puppets were based on a popular drama known as the *Commedia Del-l'Arte,* in which there were several clowns, or *zanni,* to keep the people laughing. Polcinella was a little man with a very hooked nose and chin, and a hunched back. He wore a ruffled collar around his neck and had a pointed hat with a bell.

Punch was brought to England in about 1660, and he soon became a popular character. At that time he was a marionette, not a glove puppet. Everyone loved the puppet plays because the puppeteers used them to poke fun at the authorities. By 1825 Punch had a wife, Joan (her name later changed to Judy), and the puppet stories had become firm favorites.

Make Punch

Traditional Punch characters were carved from wood, but this one has a papier-mâché head and a fabric body. The head is quite big compared to the body, but it must be light so that your hand can move the puppet easily.

To perform a traditional play you will also need to make Judy, her baby, the policeman, and the crocodile.

1 Scrunch paper into a head shape and stick it onto cardboard with masking tape. Roll a piece of oak tag around your finger and tape it to make a tube. Push tube under the paper to form neck.

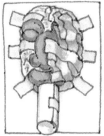

2 Push a shortened toothpick into the head so it sticks out a little. Form nose out of modeling clay and press onto toothpick. Add eyebrows, eyes and mouth. Add papier-mâché by sticking small pieces of newspaper, in layers, over the face.

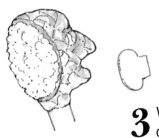

3 When dry, cut head away from cardboard. Fill back with cotton balls. Cut out two oak tag ears and stick to head with tape. Cover the back of the head with more papier-mâché and let it harden. Paint with white glue before painting features with colored paints. Apply gesso.

4 To dress Punch, cut out two fabric bodies. Pin and sew, leaving the neck and bottom edge open. Turn the right side out and neaten hem. Sew a running stitch along the edge of a strip of felt to make a drawstring for the ruffle.

5 Measure halfway around head and make a pattern for hat. Cut from felt, and sew. Cut a separate piece for brim. Cut out four hand shapes. Decorate clothes with rickrack braid.

6 Glue neck of body to head tube and tie on ruffle with drawstring. Glue hat and brim to head. Glue hands together, leaving cuffs open. Glue hands to his arms. Add a bell to his hat!

Carved wooden puppets

These African figures seem at first sight to be very different from many people's idea of puppets. They have few moving parts and are more like carved figures or masks. However, they are genuine puppets, which are used by storytellers to teach history, to tell legendary tales, and to pass on the values of the tribe or village group.

The woman puppet on the left is a Marka marionette from Tenne in Mali. The Marka, who are part of the Senoufo tribe, use these puppets to tell traditional fables. She is carved from one piece of wood, and her face and head are decorated with strips of tin nailed to the surface. Her arms are operated by pulling a string from below.

The warrior on the right, with his shield and scimitar, is from Tunisia, North Africa. He may be the same character as the Indian dancing puppet, Amar Singh Rathore, on page 6. If so, he has traveled to North Africa from India. Puppet characters often moved from country to country as entertainers traveled on the trade routes.

The warrior is a puppet with no strings. The storyteller would probably hold him in his hand and act out the story for his audience.

Make an African warrior

You will need: balsa wood for body, hands, and legs: one piece 2½ x 2½ x 16 in (6 x 6 x 41 cm), two pieces 1 x 1 x 2 in (2.5 x 2.5 x 5 cm), two pieces 1 x 1 x 18 in (2.5 x 2.5 x 46 cm) • white glue • paints • gesso • piece of wire • two washers/buttons • large sheet of gold cardboard • one piece of fabric, 18 x 15½ in (46 x 39 cm), for the skirt • two pieces of fabric, 5½ x 11 in (14 x 28 cm), for the arms

1 Mark out the puppet's features on the large piece of wood, using one corner as his nose. Grip in a vise and use a mat knife to cut out the features.

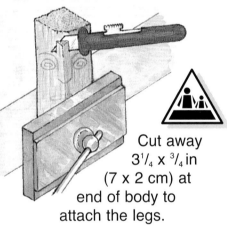

Cut away 3¼ x ¾ in (7 x 2 cm) at end of body to attach the legs.

2 Cut a 2-in (5-cm) piece off the end of each leg and glue it on at right angles, to form feet. Cut a ½ x 2½ in (1 x 6 cm) piece from top of each leg. Use knife to cut wrist shape at one end of each hand. Cut V shapes for fingers. Paint all pieces white before adding poster paint. Apply gesso.

3 Use a nail with a large head to make holes through the legs and body. Thread a piece of wire through the leg, washer, body, washer, and leg. Twist the ends so that the legs are secure but move freely.

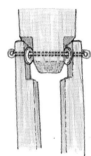

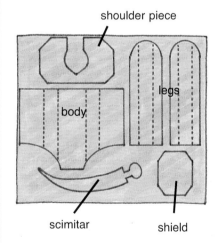

shoulder piece

body

legs

scimitar

shield

4 Draw all the pieces of armor on gold cardboard. Cut out and decorate by scoring and denting with a blunt pencil.

5 Sew the sides of skirt together and hem. Sew a running stitch around top and pull to gather. Sew down one side of each arm piece, turn right side out, and iron flat. Glue hands to arms.

6 Glue dress to waist and arms to shoulders. Wrap armor around body, add shoulder piece, and glue to back. Glue armor pieces to legs, shield to one hand, and scimitar to the other.

INDONESIA

Shadow puppets

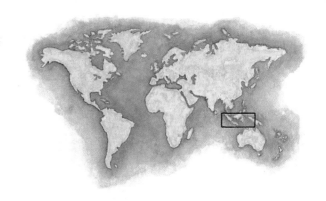

The fascinating art of the shadow puppet may have begun in Southeast Asia, and there is still a strong tradition of these puppets in Indonesia, China, and India.

Originally shadow puppets were representatives of people's ancestors, whose spirits were invited to enter the puppets. The spirits gave messages and advice on family matters or in times of danger. Today the plays are mostly seen as entertainment or ways of teaching people, but there is still something magical about the performances.

In a typical shadow theater the puppets are held against a white screen, which is tightly stretched across a wooden frame.

The performance begins in the evening, lit from behind by an oil lamp, and can go on all night. The puppet master has to be a man of many talents. He operates the puppets, tells the story, directs the orchestra, and sometimes even plays a musical instrument as well!

This is a Wayang Kulit puppet from Java in Indonesia. The word *wayang* means "shadow," and *kulit* means "skin," or "leather."

Make a Wayang Kulit puppet

You will need: cereal box cardboard or oak tag or other thin cardboard · gold poster paint · paints · gesso · a needle · paper fasteners · 3 green garden sticks

1 Draw one body and four arm pieces on cardboard. Paint your design and apply gesso.

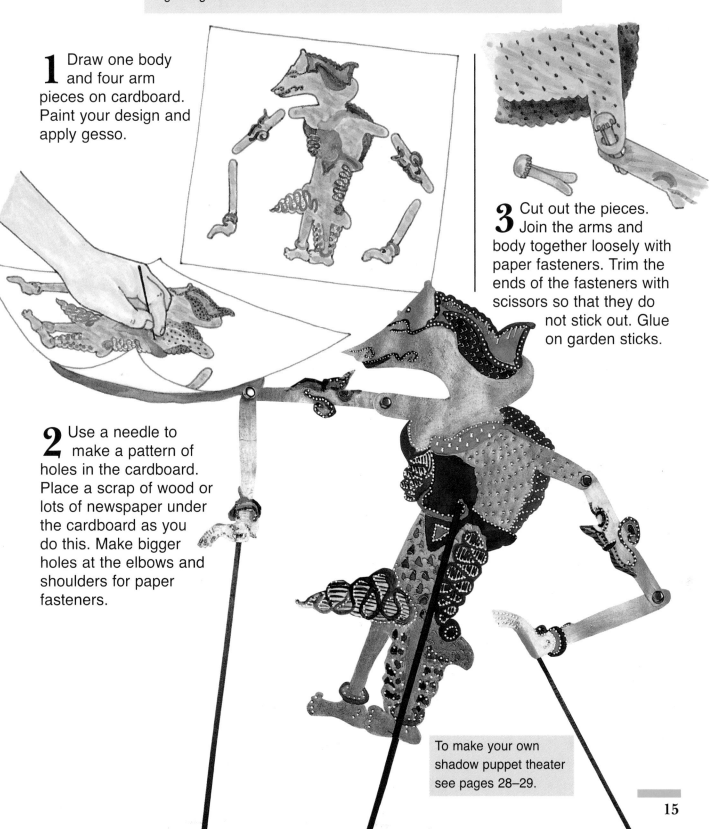

3 Cut out the pieces. Join the arms and body together loosely with paper fasteners. Trim the ends of the fasteners with scissors so that they do not stick out. Glue on garden sticks.

2 Use a needle to make a pattern of holes in the cardboard. Place a scrap of wood or lots of newspaper under the cardboard as you do this. Make bigger holes at the elbows and shoulders for paper fasteners.

To make your own shadow puppet theater see pages 28–29.

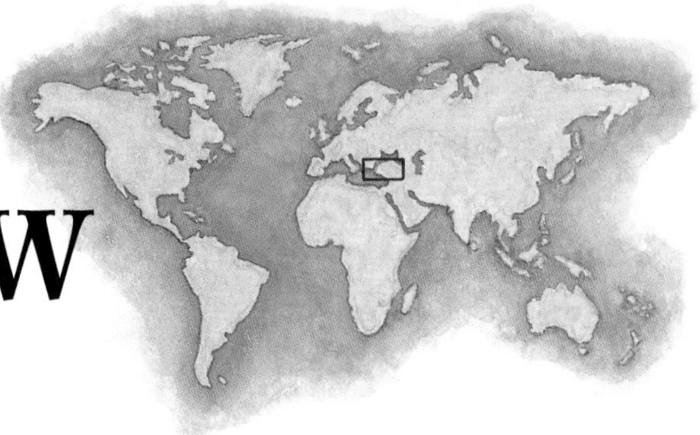

Comic shadow puppets

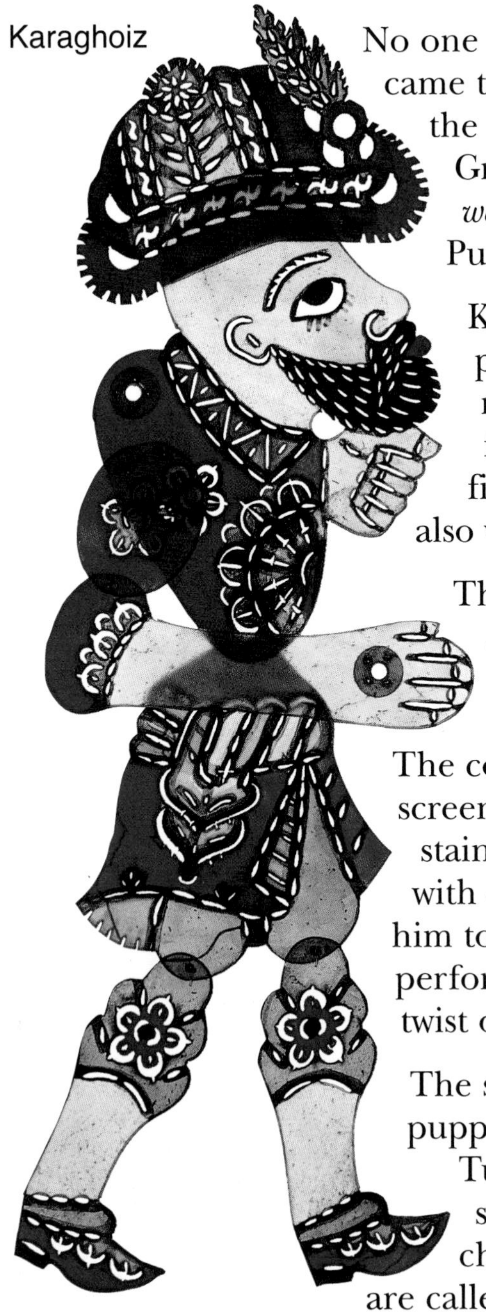

Karaghoiz

No one knows exactly how the tradition of shadow puppets came to Europe. They may have traveled all the way from the Far East via India or Arabia. These characters from Greece and Turkey are a remarkable mixture of the *wayang* tradition of Asia (see page 14) and Punchinello of Europe (see page 10).

Karaghoiz is the hero from the Turkish shadow puppet theater. He and his friend Hacivat are rough, funny characters who go in for lots of slapstick fun and fighting on stage. They are also very greedy and love food.

The plays are performed against a stretched screen, with an olive oil lamp providing the lighting. The colors show through the screen, making them look like stained glass. Karaghoiz is operated with one or two sticks, allowing him to fight, fall over, and even perform a somersault with a deft twist of the puppeteer's wrist.

The stories in Greek shadow puppet theater come from Turkey. They feature the same knockabout characters, but they are called Karagiosis and Haziavadis.

Karagiosis

Make Karaghoiz, the Turkish hero

Adapt this method to make other characters for your plays.

Make sure that Karaghoiz and Hacivat face in opposite directions so that they can talk to each other on stage.

You will need: thin white cardboard • felt-tip pens • cooking oil • modeling clay • paper fasteners • dowel rods, 12 in (30 cm) long • pencil • nail with large head

1 Draw each puppet piece faintly on cardboard. Color in with felt-tip pens. Rub oil into both sides of cardboard to make it transparent.

2 Cut out the pieces. Make joining holes by pushing a pencil through the cardboard and into modeling clay. Use paper fasteners to affix the pieces loosely together.

3 Attach the rods to the puppet by pushing a nail through the cardboard and into the end of each dowel. To store puppets, remove rods and keep in a plastic bag, so that oil does not dry out.

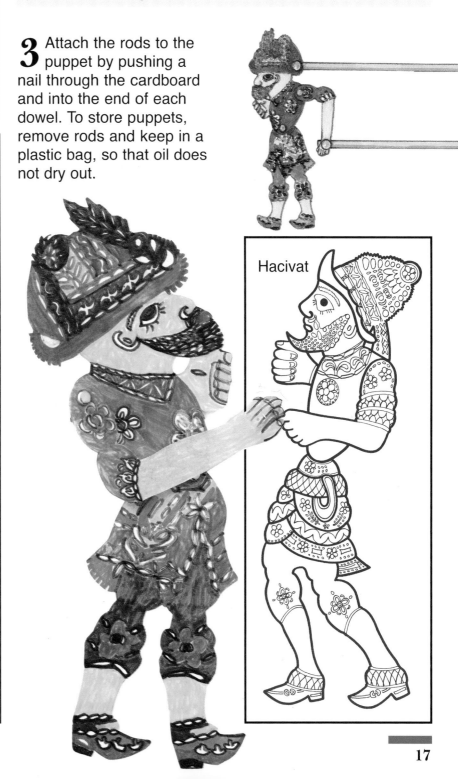

Hacivat

Rod puppets

Rod puppets are made from carved wooden pieces. The head is mounted on a long rod that passes through the body. The puppeteer moves the head by twisting this rod with one hand while moving the arms with two more rods held in the other hand. Rod puppets have long skirts instead of legs.

The puppet below comes from the Wayang Purwa plays, which tell traditional Hindu stories. Good and bad characters in the plays can be distinguished by the way they look. Even the angle of the puppet's head is important.

The rod puppet on the right comes from Java in Indonesia. She is a character from the famous Wayang Golek theater, which dates back to the sixteenth century. A Moslem Javanese ruler commissioned puppeteers to help spread the Islamic religion in Java. The plays are known as the Menak Cycle.

In Wayang Golek plays the puppet master speaks all the roles, sings, narrates, and works the puppets, as well as directing the *gamelan* orchestra.

18

Make a Menak rod puppet

1 Wrap and glue light cardboard around the end of the longer cardboard tube to form a cuff. Pierce each end of box, and push tube through so that it forms a central hole with cuff at top. Glue in place.

2 Squeeze box to form a body shape. Secure with masking tape. With dough or modeling clay mold a head onto the short tube, and hands onto two short dowels. Make small holes in hands to attach sticks.

3 When dry, paint and varnish head and hands. Wrap masking tape around long dowel until it fits into head tube. Glue firmly. Attach arm pieces to each other and to the body with fabric strips. Glue in place. Make sure arms can move freely.

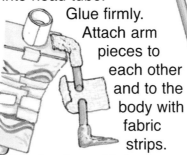

4 Cut clothes pieces from felt and decorate with braid. Sew sleeves into tube shapes. Sew jacket sides to back piece, adding in sleeves. Make a long skirt (see page 13), and tie around waist.

5 Dress puppet. Slot dowel through body so that neck rests in cuff. Tie thin string to plant sticks, thread through holes in hands, and knot. Glue short strings of beads to ears.

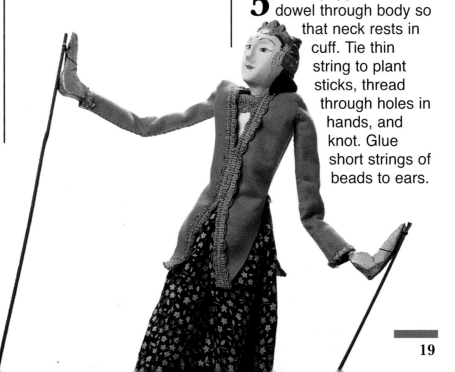

JAPAN
Lifelike puppets

Japan's *bunraku* puppets, at over 3 feet (1 m) tall, are some of the largest in the world. It takes three people to operate each puppet: one to work its head and right arm, one to work its left arm, and one to work its legs. To operate the head requires the most skill as the mouth, eyes, and even the eyebrows can move. The puppeteers wear black clothes and hoods over their faces so they do not distract the audience. The puppets wear beautiful silk kimonos, which are padded to form their bodies.

Many *bunraku* performances use stories that were written around 300 years ago. The puppeteers are silent, and a narrator at the side of the stage tells the story. Background music adds to the atmosphere. It is performed on the *shamisen*, a three-stringed instrument similar to a guitar. The musician, the narrator, and particularly the puppeteers must work together as a team. Teamwork is highly valued in traditional Japanese culture.

Make a *bunraku* puppet

This is a simplified *bunraku* puppet that can be operated by two or three people. Our puppet does not have legs, but you could have fun working out how to add them.

You will need: a balloon • newspaper and white tissue paper • modeling clay, or Sculpey, or salt dough • white glue • thick cardboard tube, 24 x 2 in (60 x 5 cm) • masking tape • piece of wood for shoulders, $^3/_4$ x 2 x 14 in (1.5 x 5 x 35 cm) • corrugated cardboard • paints • gesso • strong cloth, tape, or ribbon, 1 x 4 in (2 x 10 cm) • 2 pieces of wood for arms, $1^1/_4$ x $^3/_4$ x 11 in (3 x 1.5 x 28 cm) • 2 pieces of fabric for sleeves, 6 x 12 in (15 x 30 cm) • fabric for undershirt, 10 x 16 in (25 x 40 cm) • fabric for belt, 8 x 24 in (20 x 60 cm) • white paper • fabric for kimono, 34 x 60 in (85 x 150 cm) • 2 pieces of dowel, 24 in (60 cm) long

1 Blow up and tie the balloon. Cover with several layers of papier-mâché, leaving a hole around the knot. When dry, remove balloon. Shape face from modeling clay stuck to head. Cover with papier-mâché, finishing with a layer of tissue paper.

2 Fix tube firmly in a vise and mark a point nearly in the middle. Saw a slot halfway through for wooden shoulders to fit in. Lash shoulders and tube together with masking tape.

3 Draw around your hand on corrugated cardboard. Cut out four hands from this pattern. Glue the hands together in pairs. Paint and apply gesso to head, neck, and hands.

4 Pad shoulders with rolls of newspaper bound with masking tape. Cut two pieces of fabric tape. Glue each to shoulder and arm, allowing them to move freely. Glue hands to arms at an angle. Cover each arm with fabric glued into position.

5 Fold undershirt fabric over a rectangle of paper. Make belt in the same way.

6 Make a long T-shaped cut up the center of kimono fabric, 3 ft (1 m) long and 7 in (18 cm) across. Fold back edges and sew wide hem.

7 Put undershirt and kimono on puppet and glue to back of shoulders. Sew undershirt together at front, then the kimono. Wrap belt around and stitch at the back. Glue end of neck and push up into head so that it sticks. Attach dowels to hands (see page 19).

String puppets

These puppets are the very popular Kathputli marionettes of Rajasthan, in northern India. They are simple to operate as they only have one string, which runs from the top of the head to the back of the waist. Their heads and bodies are carved from one piece of mango wood, and their arms are made of stuffed cloth. Instead of legs the women have long skirts that swirl as they dance. Some of the men have skirts, and others have padded trousers that are bound at the ankle, with cloth feet.

The puppeteer gives his marionettes high-pitched voices by speaking through a bamboo and leather reed known as a *boli*.

The plays use many of the same themes as the shadow theater. The Hindu stories *The Mahabharata* and *The Ramayana* are particularly popular. They feature supernatural beings, gods, magical monkeys, and other exciting characters. The audience loves to see the trick puppets such as the juggler and the horse and rider (see page 26). A special favorite is the puppet with two heads — a man's head on one side and a woman's on the other. With a deft twist the man can change into a woman and vice versa, much to the delight of the crowd.

Make a Kathputli marionette

This page shows you how to make a Kathputli puppet head by carving a piece of balsa wood. This is nearest to the method used to make these puppets in India. However, you may prefer to use another method, such as papier-mâché or modeling clay.

Try making the two-headed puppet using this method. The sari for the woman should cover only half her head and hang down one side. The man could have a different skirt or trousers on his side. The second string should be attached to the shoulders to help you swing the puppet around and change its character.

You will need: balsa wood, 3 x 3 x 7 in (7 x 7 x 18 cm) • paints • gesso • fabric for arms and headdress, 8 x 10 in (20 x 25 cm) and 2 x 3 in (5 x 7 cm) • gold braid or ribbon • cotton fabric for skirt, 16 x 24 in (40 x 60 cm) • small carpet tacks • two pieces of braid, 5½ in (14 cm) long • sari material, 25 x 15 in (62 x 38 cm) • needle and two lengths of string • braid, beads, and sequins

1 Draw puppet shape on wood, using one edge as the nose. With the help of an adult, grip firmly in vise and carve out features with a mat knife. (Make body slightly smaller than head.) Sand smooth, paint white and then brown. Add features and apply gesso.

2 For arms, cut hole in center of fabric. Sew around edge of hole. Roll in short edges of fabric and join with running stiches.

3 Make smaller roll for headdress in same way. Decorate arms and headdress with gold braid or ribbon. Push balsa wood body through neck hole and secure at back with a tack. Sew or glue the headdress to the top of the head.

4 Make a long skirt from cotton material (see page 13). Secure skirt to the body with glue. Sew shoulder straps in place. Edge three sides of the sari with braid. Pin sari to top of headdress. Drape around the head and under the arms. Sew or glue at front.

5 Add strings: sew one length of string to both "hands" leaving a loop between. Sew second loop to top of head and middle of back. Decorate with nose jewelry and sequins.

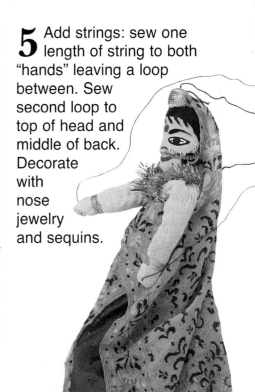

BURMA

Marionettes

This splendid marionette comes from the very strong tradition of string puppets in Burma. In the eighteenth century, King Bodawpays appointed a Minister for the Theater. Puppet performances became popular, and many plays were developed. They were a mixture of Hindu and Buddhist traditions. King Bodawpays intended the performances to be educational, as well as entertaining.

Performances lasted all night, with one play extending over six or seven nights. Some puppets had as many as fifty or sixty strings, with a movable mouth and eyes. The plays were performed on a bamboo stage, with curtains behind to hide the puppeteers. The puppets were traditionally stored on either side of the stage, the evil characters on the left, and the good ones on the right.

This puppet's white face and decorated clothes show him to be a Prince Regent. Two of these princes appear in the plays, one with a white face and the other with a red face. The prince wears trousers and a *dhoti* (loincloth), which is worn by male Hindus.

Make a marionette prince

1 Form a ball of newspaper around cardboard tube and secure with tape. Add features with paper and tape. Cover with layers of papier-mâché. When dry, paint face and apply gesso. Cut a circle of cardboard, pierce a hole in center, and glue to neck.

You will need: newspaper · cardboard tube · masking tape · papier-mâché materials · paints · gesso · cardboard disk · wood for body, 2 pieces 3¼ x 5¼ x 6 in (8 x 13 x 15 cm) · glue · eyelet · modeling clay/Sculpey/salt dough · string · thin wire · button · wood: for arms, 2 pieces ½ x 1¼ x 3 in (1 x 3 x 7 cm), 2 pieces ½ x 1¼ x 4 in (1 x 3 x 10 cm); for legs, 2 pieces ½ x 1¼ x 4 in (1 x 3 x 10 cm), 2 pieces ½ x 1¼ x 6½ in (1 x 3 x 16 cm) · colored fabric · narrow scarf · felt · wood for control: 1 piece ½ x 1¼ x 6 in (1 x 3 x 14 cm), 2 pieces ½ x 1¼ x 3¼ in (1 x 3 x 8 cm)

2 Glue upper and lower body in T shape. Screw eyelet into neck. Pierce holes through upper and lower body with knitting needle. Make hands and feet from modeling clay. Using a nail pierce two small holes in each. Paint and apply gesso.

3 Pierce hole in head with knitting needle. Fold wire in half to make needle. Knot string to button, thread through head, and tie to eyelet. With adult help, hammer a nail through each end of legs and arms.

arms

legs

4 Tie hands, arms, and upper body with string. Do same with feet and legs. Measure from hand to hand and from neck to knees. Cut out a simple fabric jacket with a back piece and two front pieces. Sew and hem edges. Cut collar pieces from felt and glue onto jacket.

5 Sew two fabric tubes for trousers. Stitch to legs. For dhoti, wind scarf around waist and between legs.

Glue jacket onto puppet. Cut star hat from felt. Glue together. Make a small hole in top of hat.

6 Make string control by nailing a short piece of wood to each end of the long piece. Thread head string through hole in hat and attach to button. Glue hat onto head. Tie other strings to puppet, and tie or loop around control as shown. To operate puppet, hold control in one hand and loops in the other.

Animal string puppets

Animals are always firm favorites in a puppet play. This lovely elephant comes from India. It is made entirely of wood, with a fabric neck to allow its head to move freely. The string controls are very simple. The elephant looks very expressive as it walks across the stage and raises its trunk.

The horse and rider appear in the traditional Kathputli play about the Rajput warrior Amar Singh Rathore (see page 6). He came to visit the court of the mogul emperor Shah Jahan, who had built the famous Taj Mahal in northern India.

Make a horse and rider

You will need: newspaper • 3 pipe cleaners or wire • tissue paper • masking tape • fabric for horse, 8½ x 12 in (21 x 30 cm) • cardboard • glue • cord for legs, ¾ x 16 in (2 x 40 cm) • beads and bells • braid, felt, or ribbon trim • ribbon or felt for saddle, 7 x 1¾ in (18 x 4 cm) • colored string, 12 in (30 cm) long • balsa wood, 3¼ x ¾ x ¾ in (8 x 1.5 x 1.5 cm) • paintbrush • gesso • felt for jacket, 6 x 1¾ in (15 x 4 cm) • felt for trousers, 3½ x 3 in (8.5 x 7 cm)

1 Roll and fold a large sheet of newspaper.

Place a pipe cleaner inside paper and fix with masking tape. Bend to form horse shape. Wrap another piece of folded newspaper and then tissue paper around the body. Fix with tape.

2 Wrap and sew small pieces of fabric around the nose and rear of horse. Wind 1-in (3-cm) strips of fabric around horse. Cut ears from cardboard. Paint and glue in bend of neck.

3 Tuck front leg cord under fabric. Stitch back leg cord to middle of horse's back. Thread beads and bells onto legs and knot. Glue braid around body. Attach saddle by stapling or gluing ends together under body.

4 Stitch colored string to head, saddle, and rear, leaving enough for tail. Wrap and glue on braid for bridle. Use beads, felt, or fabric paint for eyes.

5 With the help of an adult, fix balsa wood in vise. Shape rider's head with a mat knife. Paint and apply gesso. Twist pipe cleaner around body for arms.

6 Cut out simple shape jacket and glue onto rider. Do the same with trousers. Tie braid around jacket. Attach pipe cleaner to hand as a whip. Put the rider on the saddle.

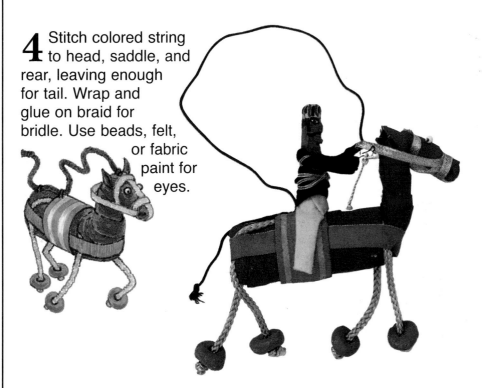

Putting on a play

In some areas of the world puppet theater is very complex, involving a whole group of people to operate the puppets, play the music, and narrate the poems and plays. Highly trained people do these jobs, and for them it is a livelihood.

However, most forms of puppet theater are produced very simply in a marketplace or a village setting, using very few props and equipment. One puppeteer does everything her- or himself, with great skill.

When you have made a puppet, you might want to perform for other people. You can do this very simply by setting up a stage to suit your needs and preparing a performance.

Before you invite other people to watch, practice by operating your puppet in front of a mirror.

A team effort

Staging a play can involve as many people as you like. You could persuade friends to play the music for you, to handle the lighting, design and print the tickets, usher the audience, or make refreshments.

You may wish to put on a more adventurous performance by getting some friends to make other characters and join you. If you are making these puppets as part of a school project, get together with everyone and decide on the best play to perform.

Making stages for your puppets

1 Cut three sides of a television-style square from a large cardboard box (the kind large kitchen equipment is delivered in). Fold and tape down to form a small stage. Cut door in side. Pin backcloths to inside back of box.

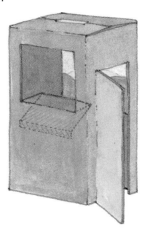

2 Lay a table upside down on the floor. Tape long garden sticks to two front legs. Stretch a length of fabric between the sticks and another between the back table legs.

A play idea for all the puppets

An emperor has a very beautiful daughter. He wants to find a prince for her to marry. As there is no one suitable in any of his neighbors' kingdoms, he sends out his horseman to give notice of a competition. Everyone is invited to come and entertain his court. The best one will marry the princess.

From far and wide the suitors come. First, the princess and her friends entertain them. Then each one performs something before the court: a song, a proverb, a story, a dance, or a fight. The princess gives each one a different colored flag to hold.

The emperor cannot decide upon the winner because they are all so good.

Finally he asks the princess to decide herself. She says that she has been so excited by their contributions that she has decided to travel the world, seeing for herself all the countries and their peoples. She jumps onto the elephant's back and rides away while everyone waves their flags and sings and dances.

If you want to make this a longer play, you could introduce some trouble. Perhaps an evil sorcerer comes to court and uses his magic powers to kidnap the princess. Then you will have to decide on a way to defeat the sorcerer and end the play on a happy note.

Glove and rod puppets need a high stage with some form of covering so that the puppeteer cannot be seen. (1.) String puppets and marionettes should have a low stage so that you can manipulate them from above. In India, string puppet operators often use a sari stretched about 3 feet (1 m) above the ground between two poles.(2.) Shadow puppets require a special screen.(3 or 4.)

---

3 Using two tables, one upside down on top of the other, stretch a tablecloth across the front at the bottom, and a white sheet across the top. Make sure the sheet is absolutely flat. Fix a small, clip-on reading lamp to back table leg. Operate puppets from behind.

4 Stretch sheet across doorway, fixing it with pushpins. Stretch thicker piece of fabric across lower part of doorway. Place a bendable-arm lamp to one side so that it throws light upward onto the back of the screen.

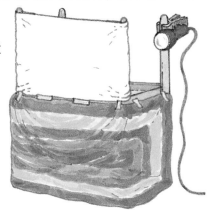

Useful information

Some helpful addresses

Puppeteers of America
5 Cricklewood Path
Pasadena, CA 91107

The Educational Puppetry
Resource Center
294 29th Street
San Francisco, CA 94131

The National Puppetry Institute
Box U-127P
The University of Connecticut
Storrs, CT 06268

The Puppet Center
32 Station Street
Brookline, MA 02146

UNIMA–U.S.A., American Center of
the Union Internationale de la
Marionette, c/o Vincent Anthony
Center for Puppetry Arts
1404 Spring Street
Atlanta, GA 30309

Equipment and materials

Most supplies are available in local
craft and hobby stores, and even
five-and-tens. You can also order
supplies through the mail.

Leisurecrafts Inc.
3061 Maria Street
Compton, CA 90224
(213) 537-5150

Pearl Paint Co.
1033 E. Oakland Park Boulevard
Ft. Lauderdale, FL 33334
(305) 564-5700

Trost Model & Craft
3129 W. 47th Street
Chicago, IL 60632
(312) 927-1400

The Brighten-Up Shop
618 Central Avenue
Great Falls, MT 59401
(406) 453-8273

S & R Distributing Co.
714 Greenville Boulevard
Greenville, NC 27834
(919) 756-9565

A Hobby Hut
2835 Nostrand Avenue
Brooklyn, NY 11229
(718) 338-2554

Pearl Paint Co.
308 Canal Street
New York, NY 10013
(212) 431-7932

Dupey Management Corp.
P.O. Box 169029
Irving, TX 75063
(214) 929-8595

Thomas Wholesale
5641D General Washington Drive
Alexandria, VA 22312
(703) 820-9790

Craf-T Inc.
P.O. Box 44577
Tacoma, WA 98444
(206) 537-5353

Tri-County Distributors
2785 S. 167th Street
New Berlin, WI 53151
(414) 782-2120

Sculpey is made by:
Polyform Products Co.
9420 W. Byron Street
Chicago, IL 60176
(312) 678-4836

Puppet theaters

The Bil Baird Puppet Theater
American Puppet Arts Council
New York, NY

Chrysler Museum Puppet Theater
Norfolk, VA

National Theater of Puppet Arts
Great Neck, NY

Pickwick Puppet Theater
Fairview, NJ

Tanglewood Puppet Theater
Brentwood, TN

The Whistle Stop Puppeteers
Monterey, CA

The Yueh Lung Shadow Theater
Jackson Heights, NY

Museums

Children's Museum of Manhattan
314 West 54th Street
New York, NY 10019

Brooklyn Children's Museum
145 Brooklyn Avenue
Brooklyn, NY 11213

Newark Children's Museum
49 Washington Street
Newark, NJ 07101

Washington Children's Museum
4954 Macarthur Boulevard
Washington, DC 20007

Children's Museum of Los Angeles
310 North Main Street
Los Angeles, CA 90012

La Jolla Museum of
Contemporary Art
La Jolla, CA 92037

Puppets for sale

Fred Cowan Puppets
Crawfordsville, IND

Larry Englar-Poko Puppets
Roslyn Heights, NY

Puppets, Fairview, NJ

Puppets With a Purpose
Spring Valley, CA

Steven's Puppets, Middlebury, IND

Books

Brown, Forman. *Small Wonder: The
Story of the Yale Puppeteers and the
Turnabout Theater:* Metuchen, NJ:
Scarecrow, 1980.

Currell, David. *Puppets and Puppet-
Making.* New York: Mallard, 1992.

Fijan, Carol and Ballard, Frank.
Directing Puppet Theater. San Jose,
CA: Resource Publications, 1989.

Fling, Helen. *Marionettes: How to
Make and Work Them.* New York:
Dover, 1973.

Flower, Cedric and Fortney, Alan Jon.
Puppets, Methods and Materials.
Worcester, MA: Davis, 1983.

Hanford, Robert Ten Eyck.
*The Complete Book of Puppets and
Puppeteering.* New York: Drake, 1976.

Marks, Burton. *Puppets and Puppet-
Making.* Boston: Plays, Inc, 1988.

Wells, Haru. *The Master Puppeteer.*
New York: Crowell, 1976.